Oakie
The Little Oak Tree
That Didn't Die

A True Story

By Melvin I Taks

DEDICATION

To all my friends and fellow volunteers that worked with me at the Cradle Of Forestry.
This beautiful national forest park iis located on the site of the first forestry school in America
in the Pisgah National Forest, North Carolina

CONTENTS

In a wooded plot near a town so small.

Grew mighty oak trees, stout and tall.

Here, the squirrels did live and play.

Collecting acorns through the day.

Some they buried in the land.

So, when winter came they'd be close at hand.

They buried so many in the ground.

Some of them were never found.

Then one day with winter gone by.
The birds had come to sing.

Where an acorn in the soil did lie.
Little Oakie, from the land did spring.

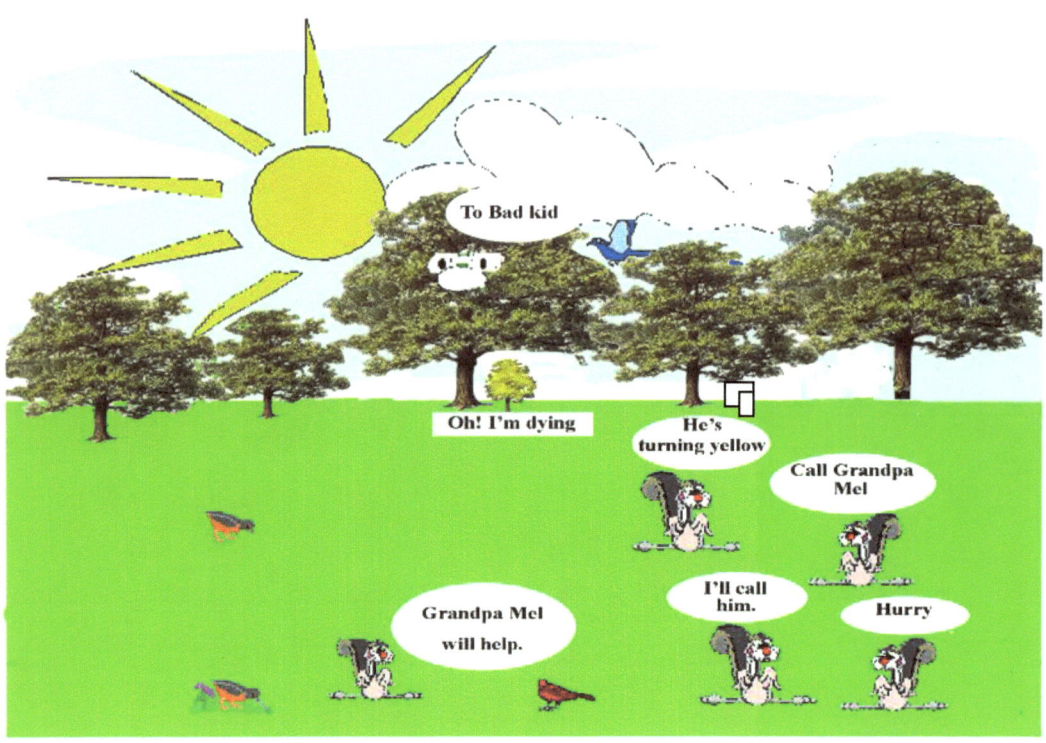

Here, many trees could be seen.
Big ones and small ones, in a world of green.

To see the sun, they would try.
Because, without its light, they would die.

As a bigger tree spread its branches wide.
The sun from Oakie it did hide.

"Oh please!" Oakie cried, "Don't do this to me."
'Tis the light of the sun, that I must see."
"Ha!" Said the big tree. "The sun does shine."
"It shines just for me." "It's mine all mine."

It was then that I came walking by.
My name is Grandpa Mel.
I knew that little Oakie, without the sun,
could not be doing well.
"Fear not, little Oakie," is what I said.
"I will go for a shovel, it's in my shed."

Early the next morning, I returned.
With a shovel in my hand.
Carefully, the soil I turned.
To remove Oakie from this land.

Alas, Oakie went into shock.
His leaves began to fall
"Oh woe," I thought, "Oakie will never live,
to be stout and strong and tall."

It was then I heard a terrible sound,
coming from that wooded plot.
They would build a house where Oakie once lived.
Why! It was on that very spot.
Bulldozers came, they crashed and rumbled.
Until all the trees broke and tumbled.

Many weeks went by, with much tender care.
Oakie grew new leaves and spread his branches in the air.

Now Oakie stands so straight and strong.
His branches reach the open sky.
In Grandpa Mel's front lawn.
The little oak tree that didn't die.

A NOTE FROM OAKIE

Dear friends,
I really hope that you may see
There are many ways to save a tree.
My love to you all,

Oakie Treebody

Native Trees
Of
North America

American Sycamore Tree

You can tell me apart from other trees by my mottled bark, which flakes off in great irregular masses, leaving my surface mottled, and greenish-white, gray and brown.

I can grow to be very big, typically reaching up to 98 to 130 ft high and 4.9 to 6.6 ft in diameter when grown in deep soils.

I am an American native and I like living where there is a lot of wet lands. I like to live in places like Iowa to Maine in the north, Nebraska in the west, and south to Texas and Florida.

One of us lived in front of Grandpa Mel's boyhood home. He used to like to play with the seed pods that grew on our branches. When you break them open you will find thousands of winged seeds inside them. If you get them inside your shirt, they will make you itch. The little boys used to call them Itchy Balls.

I enjoy providing you with my beauty, shade, lumber and fresh oxygen for you to breath. Did you know that trees are very important to your health? They help make the air pure because they breath out oxygen.

Sycamore Tree

Hickory Tree

I like living in most of the Eastern United States and you may find me living in the same forests as Oakie.

My wood is very hard, stiff, dense and shock resistant. there are some woods that are stronger than hickory and some that are harder, but the combination of strength, toughness, hardness, and stiffness found in hickory wood is not found in any other commercial wood. It is used for tool handles, bows, wheel spokes, carts, drumsticks, lacrosse stick handles, golf stick shafts (sometimes still called *hickory stick*, even though they may be made of steel or graphite), the bottom of skis and walking sticks. Paddles are often made from hickory. Baseball bats were formerly made of hickory, but are now more commonly made of ash.

Hickory is also highly prized for wood-burning, because of its high energy content. Hickory wood is also a preferred type for smoking cured meats. In the Southern United States, hickory is popular for cooking barbecue, as hickory grows abundantly in the region, and adds flavor to the meat. Hickory is sometimes used for wood flooring due to its durability and character.

The nuts of some species are good to eat, while others are bitter and only suitable for animal feed. Shagbark and shellbark hickory, along with pecan, are regarded by some as the finest nut trees.

Hickory Tree

Sugar Maple Tree

Sugar maple is a magnificent forest tree. It is abundant in North Eastern United States.

You may wish to purchase real maple syrup. It is very sweet and you may use it with pancakes or as a topping on your cooked cereal.

Besides providing beautiful borders to many miles of highway, and hundreds of thousands of gallons of maple syrup, it yields a wood of high grade. The wood is hard, strong, close-grained and tough, with a fine, satiny surface. It is in great demand for flooring, veneer, interior finish, furniture, shoe lasts, rollers, and as a fuel wood of the best quality.

Pecan Tree

I am a large deciduous tree, which means I shed my leaves in the fall and grow new ones in the spring. I can grow to 130 ft in height.

Most of the pecans in the world are produced in the United States. The leading pecan-producing state is Georgia, followed by Texas, New Mexico and Oklahoma, they are also grown in Arizona, South Carolina and Hawaii.

Pecan trees may live and bear edible nuts for more than three hundred years. The nuts are a delicious treat and are also used in the making of candy such as pralines.

Pecan Tree

www.ingramcontent.com/pod-product-compliance
Lightning Source LLC
Chambersburg PA
CBHW060818290526
45792CB00005BB/1711